Summary

of

Lundy Bancroft's

Why Does He Do That?

Inside the Minds of Angry and Controlling Men

by
Swift Reads

Table of Contents

Overview 3
Key Insights 7
Key Insight 1 9
Key Insight 2 11
Key Insight 3 13
Key Insight 4 15
Key Insight 5 17
Key Insight 6 20
Key Insight 7 22
Key Insight 8 24
Key Insight 9 26
Key Insight 10 28
Important People 30
Author's Style 31
Author's Perspective 33

Overview

Why Does He Do That? Inside the Minds of Angry and Controlling Men (2002) by domestic violence expert Lundy Bancroft is a non-fiction book for those who have experienced or are experiencing intimate partner violence and abuse. *Why Does He Do That?* outlines types of abuse, including physical, emotional, financial, verbal, and sexual abuse, and provides insight to shed light on the underlying reasons for abusive behaviors. Though domestic violence can occur in same-sex relationships and women can be abusive, the book's language refers to abuse victims as women and abusers as men for the sake of simplicity.

Anywhere from 2 to 4 million women are abused every year in the United States, causing lasting damage to the victims' psyches, self-esteem, and family structures. At least half of victims find that the emotional component of abuse is the most damaging, even when physical or sexual violence is also present.

Abusive men seek control, and at the heart of their toxic attitudes and actions is a belief that they deserve to have control. They think that their rights, feelings, and desires are significantly more important than their partners' rights, feelings, and desires. Often, abusive men create distractions, like blaming the partner or erupting in anger. These distractions are intended to prevent the abused partner from seeing a basic truth: that he feels entitled to control his partner.

According to Bancroft, there are multiple styles of abusers. For example, Mr. Sensitive is often good at talking about psychological issues and appearing to be sympathetic to his partner and women in general. However, his behaviors reveal a different reality: he will often be moody, particularly when he doesn't get his way, and ensures that the focus of the partnership is on his feelings. The Player often surrounds himself with women and likes to keep his partner guessing as to whether or not he has been faithful. His dishonesty ensures that he is always in charge of the relationship. The Water Torturer rarely loses his temper and wages a campaign of hostility, condescension, and passive aggression, so that when his partner gets upset at his treatment, he can claim innocence. Many men fit one profile, but share characteristics of others.

Abusive men have no interest in ceding control to their partners, or being in a relationship that is based on respect, equity, and reciprocity. They might offer up a range of excuses to ensure that they retain control. For example, they may become angry, and blame their abuse on their partner for having triggered the anger. However, the real issue they have is not their anger, but their partner's anger. They may blame their abuse on their difficult childhood or substance abuse problem, but in fact they abuse because they want control. Any excuses offered are meant to obfuscate the underlying dynamic, which is a need for control.

Often, remorse and promises of better behavior follow violent outbursts, but this is part of the cycle. Abuse victims often believe that if they behave correctly, the abuse will stop. Victims frequently try to be more understanding or they plead with their abusers to change. Couples therapy will not help, as this modality is intended for problems that are mutual, and requires that both partners are emotionally and physically safe. The only thing that will truly end the cycle of abuse is for abusers to know that there are real-world consequences, such as having their partner leave or facing legal sanctions.

For treatment to succeed, abusers need rehabilitation programs that specifically target their abusive beliefs. However, even those may not work. It's not uncommon for an abuser to participate in such a program and appear to be getting better, only to relapse into bad behaviors once the program is over. Real and lasting change in an abuser can only happen when there are consequences and accountability for the behavior, education about its causes, and confrontation on negative, entitled attitudes.

It's vital for women who have been abused to shift the focus to themselves, instead of trying to change their abusers. Abused women have low self-esteem and doubt their perceptions, which is precisely the outcome the abuser aims for. By focusing on their own experiences, abused women can begin to repair some of the damage and curtail the cycle of abuse. With the right support, women can regain their sense of safety and heal from abusive experiences.

Key Insights

1. Abusive men and their partners tell vastly different stories regarding the abusive behaviors that have occurred.
2. Abusive men are highly skilled at concealing their toxic behaviors.
3. Abusive men often appear to have two distinct personas, one that is caring and one that is domineering.
4. The consistent depersonalization of victims leads to an escalation of abusive behaviors over time.
5. The root cause of abuse is not that abusers are mentally ill—though mental illness might be present—but that they value control above all.
6. While most abusers are charming in the beginning of a relationship, there are often warning signs, even in the honeymoon phase.
7. Abusers try to conceal the many benefits they get from being abusive.
8. Ending an abusive relationship is challenging, but worth doing.
9. Society condones abuse against women, which is a contributing factor to the continuation of abuse.

10. The court system can provide safety, but it can also perpetuate victimization.

Key Insight 1

Abusive men and their partners tell vastly different stories regarding the abusive behaviors that have occurred.

Analysis

Abusive men use tactics of manipulation, gaslighting, and deception to paint a picture of the relationship that is far different from the reality. An abuser might project negative behaviors onto his partner, by, say, accusing his wife of infidelity while he is the one having an affair. Abusers minimize and deny aspects of the abuse to make it sound like their partner is the one inflicting harm, or simply crazy.

The abuser's efforts to spin fantastical tales are often extreme, as illustrated by the experience of Roia Atmar, whose husband poured turpentine on her and then lit her on fire. In a 2015 article in *The Guardian*, Atmar recounts how her husband told hospital staff that his wife's head scarf had caught on fire. By then, Atmar had been with her husband for many years. They had children together, and she feared for her own and her children's safety if she were to take them and leave her husband. Atmar was so beaten down by the abuse that she didn't think anyone would believe her, or care. At the hospital, her husband went to great lengths to ensure that she was never alone to reveal the truth. He spoke on her behalf. Finally, a social worker caught on to what was happening and was able to convince him to leave the room, so that the social worker could speak to Atmar alone. Atmar, heartened that people cared, accepted help from the social worker, her family, and the police, and was able to leave him for good. Like Atmar, many women feel trapped and helpless because their abusive partner tells a vastly different story from their own.

Key Insight 2

Abusive men are highly skilled at concealing their toxic behaviors.

Analysis

Abused women often report a sudden shift in the abuser's behavior if the police suddenly arrive. They are expert at controlling their image and how they appear to others. They know how to get people—such as family members, colleagues, and therapists—onto their side, which can be infuriating and confusing for the abused women.

Take the hypothetical example of Renee, a middle-aged woman married to a mild-mannered doctor, Bob. Bob is beloved in their community. He is friendly and appears to be very gentle and sensitive. Renee, however, has a different experience of Bob when they are at home alone, or with their children. Bob has never hit Renee, but he frequently makes snide comments about her lack of intelligence and sneers at her opinions. Bob may be mild-mannered with others, but Renee rarely sees this side of her husband, who is intent on disparaging her and lobbing passive-aggressive insults her way. If she ever complains to her family, her relatives are prone to believe Bob. Why wouldn't they? He is such a great, easy-going guy, or so it seems. Since they've never seen him raise his voice or cut Renee down, her relatives assume that Renee must be the one with the problem. Because Bob is consistently well behaved around others, he can't blame his abusive behavior on anger or simply having a bad day. Clearly, Bob, like most abusers, has given himself permission to disrespect his partner.

Key Insight 3

Abusive men often appear to have two distinct personas, one that is caring and one that is domineering.

Analysis

Keeping victims confused is the abused man's greatest weapon for gaining control. If his partner is always guessing what his actions mean, she can't see or call out his bad behavior. One way that abusive men create confusion is by being emotionally unpredictable. The abuser might be caring in the afternoon and extremely callous and disrespectful by dinnertime. Women frequently take responsibility for drastic shifts in behavior, thinking if they could only have acted differently, the abuse might have not occurred. This responsibility is misplaced.

NFL player Ray Rice, who was caught on video in 2014 knocking out his then-girlfriend, exemplifies the duality of abusers. Rice had wooed Janay Palmer with a new Acura and a diamond ring. The star player had a reputation as a nice guy. But the video of him punching Palmer told a very different story. If Rice was capable of charming his girlfriend, he was also capable of putting her in grave physical danger. The video led to the termination of his multimillion-dollar contract with the Baltimore Ravens. Yet Palmer stood by her man, marrying him one day after he was indicted for assaulting her. Many people following the story expressed confusion at Palmer's public support of the man who violently attacked her and then spit on her. It's possible that she could not reconcile his violence with the more loving and generous partner she knew. Palmer, like many women, may have ultimately blamed herself for her abuser's behavior.

Key Insight 4

The consistent depersonalization of victims leads to an escalation of abusive behaviors over time.

Analysis

Abusers objectify their partners, a process that helps limit the guilt and compassion they might feel for their partners following an abusive and violent episode. They treat their partner as less than human when calling them vicious names or perpetrating physical or sexual assault. This inability to see their partner as an equal human being only leads to greater abuse and violence over time. There is nothing the woman can say or do to make the abuser recognize her humanity.

Because the objectification of women is rampant in society, it may be helpful to understand what objectification looks like, as writer Melinda Miley explores in a 2017 *Thought Catalog* article. To illustrate objectification, Miley points out that people put on shoes they like, whenever they need to and at their personal whims. In an abusive relationship, the abused person is equivalent to the abuser's shoes, existing solely to serve the abuser's needs and desires. In Miley's experience, a partner who gives frequent superficial compliments about his mate's physical appearance, but shows no interest in her thoughts and feelings, is revealing how little he notices—or cares about—her substance. Miley also warns that men who objectify women may very well not be faithful. Since they view women as objects intended to serve *their* desires, they feel no guilt about swapping out one woman for another. Staying with a man like this only reinforces his belief that women are not human. If he knows his partner will accept his abuse, it often escalates.

Key Insight 5

The root cause of abuse is not that abusers are mentally ill—though mental illness might be present—but that they value control above all.

Analysis

Abusers may appear to struggle with mental health issues and in fact, they may be suffering from narcissistic personality disorder or another psychological condition. However, psychological difficulty is not the reason they are engaging in abuse. They engage in abuse because they seek full control, often by silencing, deceiving, and coercing their partners. Further, abusers believe that having their needs met should be the top priority in the relationship. Neither couples therapy nor individual therapy will help the abuser; what abusers need to change is their thinking that they are entitled to control.

Writer Bridey Heing was subject to her ex's entitlement and need for control, which she describes in a 2018 article for *The Cut*, but she still had a hard time identifying his abusive behavior as such. When they first met, she was a floundering 19-year-old barista, and he was older, in school and seemed to have his life together. Heing was eager to follow his lead, and he used her vulnerability to his advantage. When she asked his thoughts on having a serious relationship, he told her that it was immature of her to even ask. Six months into their relationship, Heing went back to school and signed a lease on an apartment. Instead of being happy for her, her ex yelled at her for not consulting him about her apartment. When she started talking about career possibilities, including overseas work, he disparaged her dreams and said that she should move with him to follow his dream job, which was located across the country. Heing, whose self-esteem had suffered in the relationship, accepted his marriage proposal and moved across the country to live with him. From there, the relationship got even worse. Heing's ex was easily set off by little things, such as not filling the gas tank all the way. His hostile outbursts kept her in a constant state of fear and worry, which is how he controlled her. Eventually, she found an online forum for brides-to-be. There was a section for women to discuss wedding-related relationship problems, and Heing anonymously confessed that she was unhappy. The response from strangers on the site was overwhelming; many affirmed that she was in an abusive relationship. As she received continued support, her ex became violent, punching a wall when she said that she wasn't in the mood for sex. Heing eventually delivered an ultimatum; things had to change by a certain date or she would leave. Her ex did not change, and so she left. Heing now recognizes her ex's behavior as abusive and controlling, but her experience of staying in a toxic relationship, despite the damage it caused her, illustrates the way in which an abuser's need for complete control can leave the abused partner confused and, at least temporarily, immobilized.

Key Insight 6

While most abusers are charming in the beginning of a relationship, there are often warning signs, even in the honeymoon phase.

Analysis

Many abuse victims have a similar story: In the beginning of their relationship with the abuser, everything was wonderful. However, even in the blissful period, there are red flags that women can watch out for, such as getting serious very quickly or speaking disparagingly about an ex-partner. If a new partner is quick to disparage her opinions or critique what she wears, these are harbingers of abuse to come.

In a 2016 article in *The Guardian*, an anonymous writer chronicled her three-year ordeal in an emotionally abusive relationship, citing the rather obvious red flags that she decided to ignore early on in the relationship. Her boyfriend sent her a barrage of angry texts one night, in Spanish, which she, as a non-Spanish speaker, couldn't understand. But by the time she'd woken up the next day, he had sent an apology. While this was clearly a bad sign, the writer was too enamored with his charming side to let the unsettling reality of his texts register. In her case, the abuse never became physical, but his intimidation tactics made her fearful of him, and of doing the wrong thing, all the time. The writer points out that early warning signs often masquerade as concern and care. For example, a man who seems very attentive and interested may lavish his new love interest with expensive gifts and talk of staying together forever. He may gift a phone, with the ulterior motive of keeping tabs and making sure that she is always accessible. Such gifts are not generous gestures; rather, they are early efforts at control.

Key Insight 7

Abusers try to conceal the many benefits they get from being abusive.

Analysis

Abusers abuse because it benefits them. They feel fulfilled by dominating and controlling their partner, and enforcing their own desires. They receive attention, control the finances, and are affirmed in their entitlement. To ensure that they continue to benefit from abuse, they distract from how much the cycle works for them.

Reformed abuser Jerry Retford had an epiphany when he saw his four-year-old son become inured to the violent fights he and his wife had; it was heartbreaking that his son, at such a young age, already accepted this behavior as normal. Retford's marriage fell apart, and he went on to other relationships. He was never physically abusive again following his divorce, but a partner called him on his emotional and verbal abuse. At that point, he decided to admit that he needed help, so he enrolled in a program specifically for violent men. Eager to help others end the cycle of abuse, Retford currently collaborates on short films to challenge stereotypes about domestic violence. He is outspoken in his efforts to get men to own their behaviors and the benefits that come from being violent and controlling. He believes that once abusers start examining what they get out of being violent, they may be able to see that, whatever the benefits, their behavior generates profound fear—and that fear is not a benefit to the partner they purport to care about. As Retford's perspective shows, it's imperative to name some of the benefits of abuse, from the perpetrator's point of view, and to gain a better understanding of how other choices would be, in fact, more beneficial.

Key Insight 8

Ending an abusive relationship is challenging, but worth doing.

Analysis

The low self-esteem that comes from being abused is one of the main reasons women stay in toxic relationships. They doubt themselves and their perceptions. Abused women also carry profound fears of what will happen to them if they finally take steps toward freedom. It's best to confront those fears, admit the reality of the relationship to trusted friends, and get professional support.

In a 2017 *Cosmopolitan UK* article, one woman anonymously shared her story of finally gathering up the courage to leave her abusive partner of nine years. When she got together with Damian, she was in recovery from having been brutally raped at the age of twenty. Like many abusers, Damian was attracted to her vulnerability—she needed him, which made it easier to control her life. When she began to feel more like herself, she started to notice how mean Damian was. He called her fat and gave her a hard time about going anywhere other than the gym. He once even forced her to ingest pills, telling her that the world would be better off if she were dead. Clarity arrived soon after, when he made disparaging remarks about her body as she attempted to initiate sex. The next day, she got up the courage to ask for a divorce. Even with a court order against Damian, he continued to break into his ex's house and steal her belongings. But the strength and relief that the writer felt from finally deciding to leave was essential in giving her the will to leave him.

Key Insight 9

Society condones abuse against women, which is a contributing factor to the continuation of abuse.

Analysis

Domestic violence has been historically sanctioned. Spousal abuse did not become illegal in the English-speaking world until the nineteenth century. It took until the 1970s for these laws to be enforced, and until the 1990s for the laws to be enforced consistently. A boy might not grow up in a home with domestic violence, but there are many popular cultural influences that condone and normalize violence against women.

Sometimes, these pop cultural referents can be used as a tool to educate teens on abuse, a perspective adopted by writer Sophie Brown in a 2011 *Wired* article on Stephenie Meyer's *Twilight* series. *Twilight* features a toxic relationship between Edward and Bella. Edward tries to control Bella's movements and threatens to hurt himself if she leaves him. In one film, he plots with another character to force Bella to have an abortion. Even though his plot doesn't come to fruition, their relationship is glamorized as a love story. Brown notes that one fan, using definitions provided by the National Domestic Abuse Hotline, found at least 15 examples of abusive behaviors in *New Moon* (2009), the sequel to *Twilight* (2008). Brown sees an opportunity to use the *Twilight* franchise to talk about healthy and unhealthy behaviors with youths. Education around abuse prevention may be limited in schools. Brown suggests that parents read books and see movies, such as *Twilight,* so that they are prepared to ask important questions. Such questions can form the basis of a healthy dialogue about toxic relationships. This could help the young person to steer clear of abuse and recognize the signs when a friend might be in a negative relationship. Cultural influences that seem to sanction abuse persist, but, as Brown suggests, they can be used to open up a positive dialogue.

Key Insight 10

The court system can provide safety, but it can also perpetuate victimization.

Analysis

Relying solely on the court system for protection is not an adequate means of addressing abuse. Not all legal professionals have a nuanced understanding of abuse. Some may be abusers themselves, while others may fall for the abuser's manipulations and deceptive version of events. Some abusers have even successfully filed restraining orders against their victims. Though the legal system is far from perfect, it can be effective when the abused partner seeks out additional support, perhaps from a domestic violence agency.

Court injunctions are not a foolproof measure to stop domestic abuse, as the 2016 murder of Darcy Buhmann sadly illustrates. Buhmann had two orders of protection against her boyfriend, Anthony Fagiano, when he broke into her Bozeman, Montana home in the early hours of the morning and gunned her down in a closet where she had gone to hide. In Buhmann's case, the orders of protection were of no consequence to Fagiano and may have even escalated the situation.

For violent offenders like Fagiano, legal consequences matter little. Police officers reported finding him smoking a cigarette outside headquarters, at which time he admitted to the crime. When asked if Buhmann might need medical attention, he casually declined, stating that she was dead. As Buhmann's story shows, not all court-ordered injunctions result in safety. Taking additional measures, such as installing a security system or moving residences, might have saved her life.

Important People

Lundy Bancroft is a domestic violence expert, speaker, and the author of several non-fiction books including *When Dad Hurts Mom* (2004).

Author's Style

Lundy Bancroft writes about the abuser's mindset from his clinical experiences as a counselor of abusive men. He shares real-life case stories from his program. The book is divided into four parts: The Nature of Abusive Thinking; The Abusive Man in Relationships; The Abusive Man in the World; and Changing the Abusive Man. Bancroft outlines the different types of abusers and is methodical in explaining how to get support and how to get the legal system involved. The last chapter provides information on how to support an abused woman. There's a comprehensive index and extensive listing of resources, including a domestic abuse hotline and books and videos that will further educate readers on the realities of domestic violence.

Bancroft takes on the cultural components of abuse. He dispels many common myths about abuse, such as that alcohol is to blame for abusive behaviors, or that all abusers were once victims themselves. Bancroft cites some cultural differences in the abuser's mindset; for example, men from Latin American countries tend to be more tolerant of their partner's talking back, but less tolerant of anything that incites jealousy. Regardless of such differences, the root of abuse is the same. There are far more commonalities than differences. He points out that neutrality, on the part of society and individuals, helps the abuser continue abusing. Bancroft is always realistic about the nature of abuse when he gives advice: the abusive man has to want to let go of control. Even if he does want to let go, it may take years, and so patience is required. Bancroft advises victims to focus on themselves, instead of their partner.

Author's Perspective

Lundy Bancroft has been counseling perpetrators of domestic violence for more than 15 years. Running a treatment program, he has consulted on more than two thousand cases of abuse. As part of his treatment protocol, Bancroft counsels abusers and confers regularly with their abused partners. The wisdom he has gleaned from the abusive mindset is the backbone of this book. He is a sought-after public speaker on the effects of domestic violence on women and children and is considered a foremost expert on why abusers do what they do. He also runs healing retreats for women who have left abusive partners and are trying to regain their lives.

Bancroft does not appear to have counseling or therapeutic credentials to support his expertise. In recent years, attendees of his workshops and other domestic violence professionals have raised serious concerns about Bancroft's exploitative behavior via online postings in a Google doc, and on YouTube. Apparently, he has a reputation for dating the vulnerable women who attend his retreats in search of healing from domestic violence.

Made in the USA
Middletown, DE
03 February 2019